Inner Space

A Search for Meaning

By

Judith Rader Snyder

For Jeanie,
my friend and
fellow lay pastor
candidate, may
God bless your
ministry —
Judith Rader Snyder

ISBN: 0-7596-9619-5

This book is printed on acid free paper.

1st Books - rev. 05/16/02

Dedication

Dedicated to my parents,
Owen and Kathleen Rader

Contents

PART ONE: Beginnings

Judith Rader Snyder

She

I cry and She floats to me
warm as Caribbean sun

nuzzles me as a cat
nudges kittens to nurse

gathers me up
lays me on a tea leaf mat

unfastens my wet cloths
bathes my skin with oil

covers me with fresh dressings
and taking me on her lap

She opens her gown to me
lifts me up to her breast

skin the color of mushrooms
nipples mauve, oozing pearls.

I suck her sweet, ready milk
enter her eyes, dark as garnets

glinting me down to lapping waves
to dolphins and sea anemones.

Judith Rader Snyder

The Miracle of Blue

My first days of babyhood,
bronchi shut and festered
my full term lungs,
air sacs shriveled,
spent balloons on sticks,
and my skin turned blue.

During days under oxygen
that January 1941, nurses
shot penicillin from needles
larger than my veins, and as
Europe fought a world war,
my lapis lazuli skin
turned bloodstone red.

In remote southern Indiana
before lab tests in England
proved penicillin effective,
moldy blue brought breath,
turned my skin rosy
and floated me up
to a Xanadu of peace.

Fanfare for Blue

My eyes caress the glass
of a lotus rose compote,
its sapphire pedestal
rooted to a maple table.

My first days trumpet
from the azure, for
my skin turned blue
from lack of oxygen.

The lotus dish tapers
to a round tympanum,
stretched for a cadence
to my once-blue life.

Peace Feeler

When you were a baby
I pinched you
our parents say
to make you cry.
I deny the charge.

The scene of the crime,
a winter bedroom,
the curtain pulled,
your barred crib
and you asleep
in a fleece blanket.

I see milk glass skin,
your clenched fists,
dark curls lifting
at each breath.

I had to touch you
even though I knew
it was wrong
so I reached in
through the slats
of the crib
and touched you.

You roused and cried
and they assumed
a Daddy's girl like me
pinched you for spite.

They expected that.
Now, when we meet
our eyes ramble.
we prowl like lions

guarding our pride
since the day
you woke
to my touch.

Dogs in the Sheep

Bark of dogs,
cries of sheep,
the family awake,
my father with his rifle,
my brothers with mop handles

and I, unarmed
running downhill
under catalpa trees
behind the barn
across the creek
to open meadow
where shouts, blows
shots in the air
turn yelps to whines
and dogs slink
into shadows
of woods.

I see the dead ewe
her belly torn
her unborn lamb
stolen from her

I shepherded her
when she chewed
rye grass
by the shallow creek

Gentle arms lead me
back to warmth
of bedcovers
as dogs howl.

Green Father

During drought, I see you still,
a farmer tugging overall straps,

a schoolboy in blue OshKosh
gritty from soil you plowed,

leaning against a picture window
mourning fields of browning corn.

Loam that once oozed wetness, burst seed
crusts now like salt on windburned lips

A picture window magnifies roots
that rise, convulse in thirst, stalks dry,

corn shucks limp as gunny sacks
your sunbaked eyes searching sky

for clouds, terra cotta face to blue
ether, neck rutted as the ground

for neither red, gold, nor blue
but the promise of green drew

you to the furrows, and emerald scythes
split your netherworld seeds

as now the promise of green
cuts through my arid soul, my father.

Judith Rader Snyder

Mother Motion

Clearing the chest
at the foot
of my sick bed
your liquid hands
drift away the clutter

You tingle me
with whispery stirrings
at the oaken dresser

the rush of air
of clothes folded
in perfect arcs

You wave me
in the flotation
of silken garments

unravel me
in skeins of white yarn

Gliding to the bed
you blanket me and range
your fingers over
my damp forehead

and standing at my side
gazing down with
half-closed eyelids
you fascinate me

though I need you moving
in my mind.

Corn Maiden

Stay away, Father warns his young girl
the winter of '47. Dagger-eyes tattoo me

yet I creep from the house, downhill
to a granary door, to the top of corn

to hear the squalls of calves
grunts of castraters in the barnyard.

The pungency of semen and blood
mixes with the clean earth smell

of harvest. I hold an ear of corn
to chinks in the corn crib wall

the silks rising, curling like black
arm hairs, grain hulls slick as sweat

on skin. Gold nuggets fall
free of the cob's brown crust.

I pull the corn to my chest
climb down from the crib

open the latch to the full
force of dawn's blunt wind

my body warmed by seed's spark
my way lit by the ear's glow.

Siblings

Summer of '44, in a porch swing,
we had our fat cheeks pressed tight,
your right cheek, my left to the camera,
grins wide, arms laid around shoulders,
stomachs crunched in wiggly revelry.

In the decades since, we embrace,
touching for seconds, grins weak,
our muscles as frayed as the edge
of this black and white photo
of siblings giggling in glee.

The School

They walk to school alone
Or in pairs and triads,
greeting this first day,
with tender skin
and mouths babbling.

At school, students find
instructors in desk chairs
who know their jobs—
teaching basic training
in survival of the fittest.

The bell rings and then
a knife descends
as vacant eyes stare,
inert minds invade
the students' heads,

passions disappearing
in the power struggle,
and as the split in
each child widens,
neon signs flash:

Impotence and frigidity,
yet, in the distance,
drums beat a cadence,
ta-dum-da-dum-de-dum,
alluring rhythms of revolt.

Pitching Ace

Mound pinwheel,
propeller

of milky streaks,
gaggle of whorled

limbs, you sky me,
a white dart

with the luster
of tucked wrist,

your eye fastening
on thunderbolts

while I bloom, splayed
on a dirt field

as the arched crowd
cheers.

Mother Relay

Cauldron of my family,
you bring the sound
of bone scrapes

as you stir around
the persimmoned kitchen,
mixing, kneading.

Your blue-veined hands
hold astute carvings,
bas-relief on flesh

like roots of old trees,
forming hieroglyphs
above the ground.

Your domed frame,
little hunchback,
shrinks each lap you make,

but you think smiles can
cancel gravity,
bright eyes the color

of sea water,
crystalline,
glistening with a rage

you pressed for years
like dried flowers
from a pine slope.

You place
the wooden spoon
the deep green bowl

in my hands; I hear
crush of vertebrae
gnash of rib

on pelvis
as your ancient
scaffold fails

and your relay ends
on the smooth
linoleum floor.

Rest still, my gnome,
your distillations
surge in me.

I supply your legs,
reach out to pass
the grooved spoon,

the deep green bowl.
I create your rounds.
This race is mine.

Spaceman

My Uncle Seth, a man of spaces
like the gap between
his front teeth

or the cavity of his mouth
as a belly-rolling guffaw
expands the room

the nest of giggles when
long arms overlap
my shoulder blades

the hollow of his voice
a booming "son-of-a-gun"
as he squeezes me

his gift, a plane ride:
Phoenix to Chicago
my first flight

so I can find
my inner space
my own outer rooms.

Judith Rader Snyder

PART TWO: Middle Passage

Judith Rader Snyder

[1]Primagravida, circa 1963

Sprawling on the floor
in labor's final lunge,
clutching the rung of a chair,
visions of motherhood lost
in wrenches of uterus
forcing the pelvis apart.

Paregoric, paregoric,
Take a dose of paregoric

When the dreaded/wanted
labor began, you phoned
the doctor and he advised,
"False labor's a waste of time,
take a spoon of paregoric
and call me in an hour."

It will make your mood euphoric,
Take a dose of paregoric

You lay on the bed in agony
as contractions grew closer
and deeper in your pelvis,
rose early to phone for help
but final pains pinned you down,
there on the dining room floor.

Perhaps your belly's hyperchloric
Take a dose of paregoric

Hot liquid scalded your legs
as your fingers searched
the spongy mass squashed
inside your underwear

---

[1] A woman pregnant for the first time.

21

and pains bowled you over,
knocking your head back.

Paregoric, paregoric
Take a dose of paregoric

Now with closed eyes, counting
seconds between your pains,
one, two, three, your fingers grip
the chair, you grunt, scream, stare
at the phone remote on its table
smiling like Alice's Cheshire.

Even Alice turned dolor-ic
downing a drink like paregoric

Time passes, five long hours
of pain, your husband arrives,
kneels and lifts you, staggering
to the car, you screaming
as the car door slams shut
and tires flap on the street.

Labor's never been historic
Take a dose of paregoric

At the hospital, stethoscopes
find no heartbeat, nurses ask
how long you've been in labor,
why did you fail to get help?
why did you wait hours?
You blame yourself.

Memory loss is prehistoric
Take a dose of paregoric

A spinal block stops pain,
forceps extract the baby girl,
perfectly formed, deathly still,

as pumps, pushing oxygen
to flaccid lungs, wheeze
out a breathy rhythm.

Paregoric, Paregoric,
Take a dose of paregoric

First Light

Oh, to explain to you,
round face, lidded eyes
why you never saw light

of day; first light needs
only the rise of a star
in the blessed east.

You missed sunrise
when your lifeline broke
away too soon; I asked

to see you when the air
quit hissing and suction
stopped pulling your throat—

too late then, for light lay dead
to you, although you remained
sturdy in your creation

First breath asks only
an open nose or mouth
and expansion of lungs

yet your nostrils, your throat
closed down, voice silent,
your lungs virgin

untouched by smog,
pollens or dust mites,
and in the delivery room

your face shone deep red
like banked embers,
the color of the redbird

perched in my magnolia tree
or the hummingbird
feeder beside the window,

and now, crunch of red apple,
crack of smoldering log
bring me your sound,

your disembodied voice,
your mute desire,
your unspoken word.

Judith Rader Snyder

To a Daughter

My love, you bathed my soul with joy
when you were born, a shore
the Savior knew to quell the pain
of stillbirth thirteen months before.

You came to Earth with solemn squints;
you tugged at life and challenged me,
"What's this, why's that?" your voice
insistent in its constant plea.

Mired in my own insecurity,
I managed to hide distress
stuttered out some reasons,
gave the rest a hasty guess.

My mid-teen mothering, when I
soothed my baby brother's cries,
revealed no key for you, since he
sought peace by gazing in my eyes,

but you reached out to coax a voice,
your face upturned in tortured grace,
high cheek bones commanding awe,
bronze hair an aura framing space.

I strained to find a healing word
to fill the void you knew was mine,
and then a second baby came;
my duties cut my listening time.

Your beauty grew with later years,
your voice could sing a fluty tone,
your face had steely blue wide eyes,
an upturned nose with chiseled bone,

a face turned up to me in pain,
"Do you really love me, Mom?"
Surprised, I said, "Of course I do!"
eyebrows creased, reason numb,

and when you asked the tenth time
I faced your dad's complacency;
"Just why is she so insecure?"
He shrugged his feelings free.

But I resented being nudged
and when you agitated me
my voice sent out a weariness,
questions stopped, and now I see

your challenge brought me down
to earth, where I felt the agony
of guiding fear into light of day,
exposing my need for integrity.

Little Runaway

You stood before me at five
years old, with sad green eyes,

clothes tied up in a hanky,
saying, "I'm going away."

When asked why, you'd say,
"I don't belong. I'm adopted,"

and leave it at that, as if
God decreed that truth to you.

"Why do you feel that way?"
I asked then, and you

would say you could tell—
the way you looked different

from your sister, and no denial,
no love or reason made you empty

the clothes in your hanky bag,
and yet, the smell of my cooking

kept you close: the odor
of fried chicken, beans, potatoes

drew you to stay in our kitchen
at least until after supper.

Then darkness came
and you paused, saying,

"I guess I'll leave tomorrow."

This recurred, oh, ten times,

as years passed and then
you lost your need to run

just when I felt
the need to escape the life

I led, whether by plane,
by ship, or through daydreams

I ran until, spinning in circles,
I became dizzy and nauseous.

You watched while I
followed the same bluesy path

you took, and yes, you were there
when I stumbled into myself.

Glass

My china cabinet overflows with glass—
depression glass, cut glass, milk glass, glass
that shimmers, cools, and tingles to the touch,
the smooth, carved surfaces of figurines
that feel sturdy, yet smash when hit hard.

Glass reminds me of my grandmother,
my father's mother, tiny, just four feet ten,
as osteoporosis made her stoop and shuffle,
in pain so excruciating, she died suddenly.

After the funeral, we met at her farmhouse
and my aunts divided her things, mostly dishes;
I was given three glass pieces my aunts said
my grandmother would want me to have.

The first, a cut glass necklace, was graded,
the largest bead in the middle, the chain
broken, so I spent many hours fixing it,
cleaning the tarnish, and restringing beads.

I love the fractured light off its many facets,
and when my daughter married, she wore it
during the wedding, as the something old
a bride wears; I saw how dear it was to me.

The second piece, a small, deep, green bowl.
was placed with my mixing bowls, where I
could touch it often, its green glass the color
of the grapes outside grandmother's window.

The third dish, a curved round relish bowl,
has three eagles equally spaced on the edge,
wings out, long feathers on heads and wings,
short wavy feathers on breasts, pedestal legs.

Grandmother's soul rests inside the eagles;

I see her spread her wings and the light
bounce off her in all directions, as silently
she soars, she rises, transfigured in glass.

Annunciation

The voice insists:
"Can you wake up?
Open your eyes, Judy"

I peek out
of anesthesia stupor,
see my surgeon,
his green-capped head
hanging over mine

"I had to take the breast.
The tumor was malignant.
You're doing fine."

I close my eyes,
"malignant" slithering
behind my eyes, along
with phrases, echoes,
a vision of the doctor,
his red hair, urgent eyes

"Had to take...breast.
Fine, Fine, Fine."

I hear the words
swing like church bells
over my head
backward
forward
until a merciful
unconsciousness
blocks them out.

Time

In winter
time hangs
point down
like icicles
under eaves

or a pendulum
in a junked
antique clock

until children
sit in a circle
on the carpet
throwing dice

rattle and click
rattle and click
sevens, elevens
and snake eyes

the sound
of water drips
in small
hypnotic plops.

Judith Rader Snyder

Wind

Wind howls down
the pad-locked houses
cuts circles through weeds.

Alley strays dog my feet
click paws on pavement
drum jazz to the meter of sleet.

I prowl the beer can gutters
wheezing, coughing
lips tight over teeth

stumble onto the hull
of a wrecked
school bus

crawl inside curl up
my spine a rope
from head to pelvis

face to knees
back to metal
tight as a nautilus.

Bound to a rack
of Arctic air
I shiver there.

Silences

This afternoon
a herd of cattle
comes to drink
from an algae-
covered pond.

They stretch
ductal necks
submerge
shovel jaws
skim off
a green soup.

The mossy curtain
below the surface
of the lake parts
and water clears,
exposing soft
clay beds

tender as flesh
cut open for surgery
or insides of mouths
ajar after years
of silences.

Judith Rader Snyder

A ROUND OF MOTHERS

Judith Rader Snyder

1. Mother Alchemy

She mines vermilion—cinnabar
revives Mt. Etna's smoldering fire

The crimson river of molten mire
flowing down to a ritual fire

Her hood, an undulating cowl
awakes the sleeping dog to howl

His warnings to the unaware:
nightmare walks in midnight air

She sees me, takes my head and flings
me sideways through the eddied rings

Of planets, circling galaxies
fighting wings and clashing seas

Then calls me back, my eyes still wide,
she opens her cloak, pulls me inside

My hands and face securely pressed
against Her ribs and flattened breasts

She guides me with a birthing rope
and touching fire to pores of hope

She slides me through the birthing vein
till waiting fingers ease the pains

She salves me with Her tears and dries
me with Her cloak, then hears my cries

My whining to the patient Crone

who drew me from the dross of stone

She leaves me by a glassy pool
a funhouse mirror that mocks a fool

I reach to touch the shining well
but fingers break a mercury jell

Globes cascade, voices call,
say kings of night will give me all

Their gold, while on the other side
a Carpenter wants me for a bride

and in between a shiny orb
turns into worms my pores absorb

I take the Light, I bless the grass
the worms, the hell, the human mass.

2. Dream Mother

Her eyes rest
on roundness

Rose attar perfumes
the spoon of Her neck

In Her lava tube
stalactites drip
stalagmites hum

Cymbals slice
the webbed pulp
of time's pumpkin

Chalky watchers
sit rock still
hearing with skin
smelling with eyes
tasting with noses
seeing with tongues

Her fine-cut
fingers mat gold
orange and red
silk scarves
till design
holds mind
entranced

She spins
a reeled
round
saga
out.

Judith Rader Snyder

3. Mother Jabberwocky

You say she jabbers
this nag who weasels
her way into your play

Her voice chirrups
straining to be heard
above your curses

You shove her away
but she bites
your writing hand

Can you draw the pen
across the page
with bruised metacarpals?

Her jaws pop
maxilla from mandible
upon hearing abuse

Hold your scorn.
Her clawed feet
scratch back to you

and her cluck outlasts
your apoplexied
vocal cords

She wants an audience
and will be heard
now or after death.

4. Mother Contraire

Small wonder
your blood pressure
rises at moonfall:

you defy duty
splendidly,
your pregnant home

a Venus of Villendorf
great with keepsakes.
Offspring taunt you,

yet you sacrifice,
dropping canopy.
The falconer calls:

you writhe in spasm,
flay the nubile wind,
shudder out a mystery.

5. The Great Mother

I come to liquefy the fields
of weeds and thorns, where blooms
should suck the sun's full rays
and butterflies and bees consume
the sap of plants, wings fluttering.
Yet all lies dead now in a tomb

for nothing quickens in the womb
of soil until my fingers pull the bow
of life and guide the arrowed sperm
to split the seed's protective coat,
and zygotes never form until
my dews caress the embryo.

Seeds cannot absorb or grow
when blocked by stone above
the earth and minus nutrients
and minerals that give the grain
its rudimentary shoot, scorning
nature's path, spurning a mother's pain

so I release my love with rain
to drown your barren parentage,
but rescue seeds that cling to roots
beneath the flood, endure this age
until fire can forge the key, unlock
the womb, and end maternal rage.

6. Song of the Mother

"Loo-la-low, loo-la-low
loo-la-loo-la-low."
I nestle, content
to hear Her lament:
"Loo-la-loo-la-low."

A large hand
with iron fingers
compresses my shoulder
muscle like a band
of baling wire.

Then pincers nab
the tendons of my neck,
iron clamps
yank my head back,
a voice says, "Beware!"

I can not see
but sense the hand
is one that bans
the cosmic bliss
She feeds with craftiness.

I argue, forlorn:
"You punish me
for finding deity
in female form
but You created need

in us and said, 'Feed
my sheep;' yet men
secrete no food,
and newborns express
the milk of her breast.

We learn music
in amniotic waves
that leave engraved
in our memory
everlasting melody.

Our tissues hum
the same heartbeat
our mothers drum,
the pluck and strum
our sucking jaws repeat.

Both in her nest
and at her breast
we gain reverence
and practice for
maternal dance."

A second fist
joins in to strangle
me, and an angry
voice hisses, "Witch!"
and "Heresy!"

My struggles fail,
my heartbeat slows,
but I hear the wail
of Her "Loo-la-low,
loo-la-loo-la-low."

I lunge and gasp
and hum along,
I wheeze and hack
my Mother's song,
"Loo-la-loo-la-low."

The deadly grip
Relaxes, slips,

so now I know
I can conquer foes:
"Loo-la-loo-la-low."

Sourcery

The heart grabs me.
I try to pull away
but it is determined,

pushing me into vessels
auricular, ventricular,
murky, slimy life blood.

Faster, faster I go
into passageways unknown,
into darkness so complete

I become a pulse,
one with the heart of all,
one with the pulse of all,

One with the source
of relentless rhythm,
never to be denied.

The Harp Retuned

It wailed, a sound insistent, thin and sharp,
an out-of-tune constricted harp
unused for years, with curving body lines
to mask its stale remains of warp.

Once more I made its crusted pegs revolve,
unlocking chords of my resolve
to play the tunes, to sing each woman home
and help her fears and bonds dissolve.

I heard the tones untangling muddled thoughts;
the unison of shoulds and oughts,
I felt the dread the female artists sketch,
I held the pedestal of naughts.

God tightened down the silvery tuning key
and stroked the ancient lyre till free,
then well-tuned voices drew the sisters forth
to find empowering harmony.

Judith Rader Snyder

The Resurrected Loom

I deserted weaving when I resigned
my seat before the loom, a project left
with shuttle hanging mummy-like, entwined
within a yawn, the threads of warp and weft
held tight in a pattern of terminated lines
and faded colors, a canopy of dust
obscuring a surface of incomplete designs,
results of years of sloth and wanderlust,
treadles stopped while scrawny spiders grew
a lace-locked cage to mock my idler's game;
long years have passed since I withdrew
my hands and feet from that entangled frame,
but now I clear the crust from fabric's grain
and single-minded, weave my cloth again.

Seining for Sound

I cast a net to find a word
and heard a drone the locusts whirred

an ebb and flow, a chirr of sound
that tugged me hard and turned me round

to the reel of the summer cicadas racket:
ta-brack-e-ta-brack-e-ta-brack-et

crescendo diminuendo, a simple strain
it quivered the oceans in my brain

I drew in my net, a salty line,
and found a lover's valentine.

The Blemished Fig

My dark lover shows me a fig,
an ochre teardrop, scalloped,
with a worm hole at the side,
he holds it up to my face,
his index finger pointing to
the blemish, while a worm
waves out of the opening,
traces his milky path on
the fig's skin. My silent
lover tosses his palm out,
asking me, should he toss
it away, and I say, no, we
must keep it, then the fig
turns transparent—I see
the inner pulp, down to
the center point, the
network of tunnels,
caverns, dark and
light flesh, and as
I breathe on it
warmly
my love
takes me
in his arms.

Shower Vision

I run hot, add cold
undress, adjust again,
switch to shower
go through sliding glass,
a baby carried to bed,
blissful in steam.

Droplets hit ankles,
knees, thighs, pelvis,
chest, neck, face,
skin drooling
sensuousness.

I close my eyes
throw back my head
then turn, repeat.
Surge pummels
the tense flesh
of shoulders.

Behind my eyes
dim aura forms,
then a mass
of bent threads
that pair to make
crosses, writhing
meshing, building
a trellis

A center point
opens to
blackness
a hole
that breathes
expands

contracts
radiates
and I say:
Yes.
Beautiful.
It is good.

Conjugation

These days apart
your brown eyes
plunge like fangs
into mine

I choke on
my liquid need
for you

Your pupils
release swirling
white-hot words:
amo, amas, amat

My hog-tied tongue
conjugated
swallows free.

Indelible Image

I stored your body in
the album of my mind
memorizing every curve
and every straight line
the contour of your head
the frame your straight
brown hair makes round your
face over ear tops layered
in back almost to the shirt
around the neck that holds
a deep voice, supports your
supple face, the chin cupped
to lips that part to reveal
straight mother-of-pearl teeth
a moustache above your upper lip
that stretches wide when you grin
bunching cheeks with dimples
setting off the straight plumb
line of your nose and flaring
nostrils as you engage my eyes
with ebony pupils, brown irises
and white globes in rounded lids
below arched eyebrows, forehead
partly covered by hair tapered
softly above strong shoulders
long arms and gentle hands
with tufts of hair on the
backs and a full chest
and slimmer waist
but strong hips
held by long
running legs
that pursue,
pursue me.

A Conversation with My Daughter

You sit with me
while I speak,
hurling one-liners
in response

hating the drip,
drip of words
that carve our
crevices, etch
our surfaces.

Our eyes turn
to the lake,
to the farthest edge
where we look
for splash,
for ripples.

We wait
in silence
for drops
to fall.

The Parable

His name was Rick and he
was my pastor, with clear
blue eyes, an earnest
voice and wise mind
from his walk with God.

We discussed the meaning
of truth that day inside
church walls, our points
differing, yet both of us
pleased with ourselves.

"Stupidity!" a voice said,
and I turned to the sound
from outside the walls,
from a distance and place
eye and mind do not see.

The word washed waves
across my mind and held
me stunned, without voice,
only with ear to hear
the mysterious word.

Rick eyed me strangely,
moving away, puzzled
as I struggled to escape
the hypnotizing voice
by joining women near.

I felt a force bend
my head and body
to the floor to see
Mary and baby Laura
playing with puzzles.

"She wants to finish,
but can't," Mary said,
and when Laura cried,
Mary guided her
to place each piece.

I knelt on the floor,
grateful that words
and powers transfix
until parables show
us true humility.

Judith Rader Snyder

PART THREE: Conclusions

Judith Rader Snyder

Tortoise Time

Two taps on glass and you
appeared, two taps, you left.
Two days you roamed in my
back yard, two nests, two bites,
two nights' unease that started
Friday afternoon at dusk.

I thought a bug had hit
the pane of my patio door,
your first tap sounding light;
you knew my need of twos
and tapped again, so I rose
and found you on the sill,
your bowl shell on your back,
yellow dots spattered on
your leather neck, your claw-
bent legs, your beggars' head
a pump handle primed and set,
waiting for the pumper's hand.

As I opened the door beside
the roughened concrete patio
your sprawl brought back a scene
from twenty years before
when my daughters, babies then,
were belly-scooting on the floor
with heads like periscopes
and eyes like beacons on ships,
so I bent and picked you up.

I called you a turtle, but later
found you're really a tortoise,
marveled that your head poked out
even though my fingers traced
the ridges of your carapace,

while you clawed air to bring
a sense of ground to space.

Placing you down outside,
I laid a plate of meat
and bread in front of you
filled a plastic tub with water
improvised a ramp
but when you left the food
I followed you, awed that you
could move so fast on short legs
that see-sawed through the grass
until you reached a log
propped up on my back fence
and crawled into the hole
between the log and soil
where I could see you sit.

I came inside but felt
as if I'd lost a child,
had a vision of my cat's
last days, when she would sit
in solitary pain, refusing
to drink and or eat until
we had to end her life.
That night I dreamed of empty
space beneath the log.
At daybreak I saw my dream
was true, cleaned up the mess
outside my door, but soon
I heard two taps and felt
such joy to see your head.

I explored the food that sat
on refrigerator shelves,
saw a cantaloupe, cut a slice
and slid it beneath your mouth
where you caught the melon scent,
clamped your jaws around

the soft fruit flesh and pulled
a small chunk out, leaning
your head far back, enjoying
all the spongy, juicy meat
before it slid down your throat;
again you sank your teeth
into the orange pulp and left
a second hole, savoring
every drop as if you fed
on manna, then satisfied,
you turned away, wagging
back to your tree trunk home.
I picked up the melon slice
and laid it in your path,
but you left what you'd enjoyed
only seconds earlier and wedged
beneath the log, so I left.

I found some books to help
me understand your ways,
saw your name, Texas tortoise,
how you can outlive humans,
that your fetuses look like ours,
then visited a pet store,
saw eight tortoises in a cage
and knew I had to leave you
free and give you cantaloupe
and vegetables, even if
you took just two small bites.

I filled a low flat water trough,
placed it there beside the log
(you use your jaw to ladle,
your tongue's too short to lap)
and trusted you to find food
among the bugs and slugs
that crawled in my backyard.

The night in bed I felt

unease so I rose and went
outside, using a flashlight
to guide me as I walked
in the wet St. Augustine,
but then saw a frog blocking
my way and staring at me
so tortoise-like that I
went back to bed, relieved
to find a guard for you.
When I awoke the next day,
I feared you'd left, so I went
from room to room, window
to window searching for you.
I spotted you crawling down
a narrow strip of grass
beside my house, and as
you saw my face you stopped
to hold my gaze, your eyes
dark hollow question marks,
perhaps deciding then if my
desire could equal your own.

When I dressed, I found a patch
of purple leaf beside the house,
and a dent that formed your bed.

Then my daughter called to ask
me to shop with her, so I left,
but later, when I came back,
my husband said you knocked
two times at the patio door,
he'd looked outside but had read
his books and then I knew
you'd left, yet I raced outside
to the fence, searching from log
to purple leaf, realizing how rare
you were and how miserably
I'd failed you, how hopeless it was
to find you there in my yard.

Now two months have passed;
the log and empty hollow wait
while new leaves grow to hide
the mat that formed your bed.
When I reach in beneath
the purple foliage I
can barely feel the nest
your body made while lying
there and in the brown,
decaying leaves I see
the eyes that held my own
with such desire but left
me wanting, needing more.

Heart Attack

My brother's heart
stopped suddenly,
as if a snowstorm
swept a live wire
off its crucifix
in white Vermont,

the gush-swish
of his heartbeat ceased,
expansion gone,
contraction in limbo
as he lay grounded,
dangerous to touch.

His pulse resumed
at last, his blood
brackish at first,
restored as he
lay silent, caught
in a deep sleep.

I clutched his hand
from miles away,
willing his pulse,
connected only
by phone cables
and loved voices

those seven days
before he woke,
his heart revived,
his will to live
strong, this brother,
this necessary man.

Sunset: South Padre

Waves drag sand
from the shore
as we walk barefoot
late in the shallows
tugged by undertow,
our toes clawing
shifting seabed,

arms and legs caught
in headwind, hair back,
eyelids half-closed,
heads up to watch
clouds turn, to feel
skin bathed
in bloody dusk.

As an encore,
white light tongues
at us from under clouds
then flickers once
and slithers past
the far edge
of the Gulf.

Judith Rader Snyder

Clouds

Strong breezes
swish leaves

push eyelids
lower and lower

lashes flutter
and tingle

shadows fade
into drab ground.

In the sky
merging clouds

form a feathery
masterpiece.

The Lighthouse

The road is dusty with deep
tracks etched in its bed.
A heavy truck has left
two columns of tread.

No truck to be seen,
but a lighthouse stands
and grasses dance beside
my path, stems deep in sand

with heads bent seaward,
where salt sprays enfold
the tower and guide
me on toward my goal.

I bend against the wind
down a road lined in sedge,
to the rocks piled like seals
near waves' lapping edge,

surf caressing their sides,
shimmery as pup's down.
How many boats steered
clear of reefs around

your bay, and how many vessels
avoided being drowned
when your beacon kept
them from going aground?

You remain silent and still
until darkness brings you life.
Shine strong, then shine bright;
many sailors need your light.

71

Beat Generation
(after Raymond Carver)

Yes, we scream,
my partner and I,
we scratch, wear shades
to hide the purple welts,
the bloodshot eyes.

Your brown eyes search
the walls of my kitchen,
your thick tongue mashes
down the narcotic taste
of apple dumplings.

You turn away,
reluctant to touch me
or my doughy fingers,
trying to ignore bruises
on my arms and face.

A fly lands
on the table between us,
takes a crumb, nibbles,
then rubs its front feet
as if to raise a spark.

You avoid my gaze
by staring straight ahead
painfully, seeing my will
is weak, and yet, if I leave,
a woman takes me home.

Swamp Creature

Leeches cling
to my skin
sucking energy

moss grows
in arm pits

beetles find
a cesspool
in my navel

snakes crawl
between toes
circle thighs

while crows
build nests
in hair

Bees comb
waxy hives
in my ears

as worms crawl
through my nose
into a stomach
which churns
and sloshes

and I swell into
a giant cadaver
ready to explode.

Letter to George

Dear George,
or Mr. Scarbrough
as I knew you
at school.

You may not know me,
a shy pre-teen girl
in your English class
during 1953 to '55.

You preferred
my older brothers,
though at times
you noticed me

and as you taught,
your eyes spoke to me;
I heard mutterings,
parents leery of you.

You left, and I wrote you
an unsent letter asking you
to let me live with you—
imagine my state of mind,

but the letter disappeared
in the Indiana farmhouse
in 1962 when I married
and moved to Texas

but that summer of '55
when you returned
to Tennessee I knew
how rare you were

but not as I do now,
tumors strangling lungs,
the acid of cancer
burning my tongue

with Poe's madness,
Dickinson's loneliness,
and Thoreau's ire
my ghostly shadows.

I hope you are well;
if not, remember Dylan:
"Do not go gentle into that
good night,/ rage, rage..."

Death of a Puppy

It stood on the curb, its tail
brushing air before it darted
into the path of my car.

As bumper and tires hit
her tiny body, I heard
a sound like the bounce
of a rubber ball and saw
in my rearview mirror a furry
dervish circling a tailspin.

As I stopped my car,
a young boy dashed
into the road behind,
in heavy traffic, gently
raising the body in both
hands, the pup sagging,
limp as rolled pie dough,
drooping over his fingers.
After laying the body down
in grass, he ran for the owner.

The pup squealed as I knelt
beside it, its eyes flared,
its thin jawbones stretched
wide apart, then wider yet
as if it wanted to consume,
over the sculptured ridges
of its palate and over a wet
tongue, all the rest of its life.
I wanted to lift it in my arms
but a gurgle inside the throat
warned me that a gush of blue
blood welled around the tongue,
and as the tapered throat filled,

the puppy's eyes glazed over
as if covered by a sheer fabric
delicate as ashes floating by
in a column of smoke.

The owner ran from her house,
and I apologized, she nodded
and cradled the still body
on her chest, rose and turned
away, blue drops oozing out from
the pup's clenched, comb-like teeth,
staining her shirt and dripping
down onto stiff St. Augustine grass.

Judith Rader Snyder

Lips

I read silently
my eyes sliding
across a parquet
of type on page.

Letters glide
across my teeth,
goading lithe
tongue muscles,
shuddering
my glottis.

Vowels,
consonants
raise, press,
slide down
the back hump
of the tongue,
stimulating,
fascinating,
the throat's
watery eye.

Cattail in Autumn

Swamp candle,
velvet-headed
sentinel of sluiceways,
sepia nap blanched
by autumn chills,
you hover unlit,
camouflaged
by reeds
and rushes
where minnows
and craw-dads
meander.

Wind opens
your milky finery,
ferries gossamer
seeds skyward
and you magnify
times ten thousand.

Mere Anarchy
The L. A. Riots

Tire tread mashes
on sooty avenues,
cushions a stop
as police cars
disgorge cops
crouching,
guns up.

Store fronts
vomit glass,
thieves dodge
down alleyways,
arch their torsos
around prized
contraband

flames smear
headlines
on front pages
of L. A. Times,
lit and tossed
through spikes
of broken panes.

Another store
burns down:
Loss in Millions.
Workers pull
dead bodies
from ashes.
Meanwhile
a corner preacher
waves his Bible,
prophesying

rapture,
foretelling
the return
of Christ.

What She Feels Her Last Night

A knife at her throat,
her blood on the blade
smells of the foundry

Where steel flows red
His breath scalds her cheek
he hisses, Freeze!

Her teeth grind down
to a bitter powder
that coats her tongue.

She feels the life
inside her womb, the amniotic
fluid pressing her cervix

and senses a heart
straining to beat,
feels the frog kick

of legs that will not climb
the tree whose branches
arch over her body.

As leaves rattle overhead
she struggles in vain against
his last, sharp cut of steel.

Who Am I?

I am a crone who is proud of her age
I am a worker who earns her wage
I am a woman realizing my worth
I am a midwife helping with birth
I am a surgeon advising the intern
I am a daughter struggling to be born.

I am a mother pushing my child out of the uterus
I am a teenager remembering pain of first intercourse
I am a preteen mother remembering the anguish of incest
I am a pregnant teenager learning about condemnation
I am a single mother supporting her children
I am a college woman encountering date rape
I am a working woman harassed by male co-workers
I am a female boss resented because of her womanhood
I am a female artist whose work is called pornographic
I am a poet whose work is criticized as too womanish
I am a victim of violence from a woman-hating man
I am a doctor treating a wounded victim of violence
I am a girl devalued by parents because I am female
I am a girl baby who is drowned because she is female
I am a welfare mother who is condemned by rich people
I am a working mother who lacks decent childcare
I am a girlchild who is home alone without childcare
I am a working mother who has children home alone
I am a woman who dies in childbirth in 1838
I am a woman who was burned at the stake in 1438
I am a woman who gives birth in a prison
I am a woman who is raped by guards in a prison
I am a woman giving birth to a child conceived by rape
I am a woman proud of her handicapped child
I am a woman who loves my mixed-racial child
I am Demeter searching for kidnapped Persephone
I am female creativity, proud, fertile, working myself free.

The Shaman

Menopausal woman, lying flat
on the ground, there's a man
with bongos and stethoscope
dancing between your thighs.

He laughs, and when you moan
he scatters his capsules toward
your mouth, while you squirm
to the throb of his drum.

You cry out and he, with mouse
eyes wide, minces toward you,
oscillates his stethoscope,
a lasso that whips and spins

and pounds on the drum head,
his moustache twitching
as he chants his song,
"Make much of time!"

"Gather ye rosebuds!"
He tells you that women
over fifty turn to statues
and fall like Venus to ruins.

Something breaks his hold
over you, the twang of "ruins,"
the tilt of his chin, the smirk
on his face as your teeth grind.

Now, you carefully slide
your hand along the ground,
half-inch by half-inch, gathering
the fallen capsules in your fist,

and when he falls asleep,
you toss the capsules in
his open mouth, take his drum,
his stethoscope, and leave.

Three Sisters

Centuries, we lay apart
our unperceived signals
bounced off ancient tombs.

In glassy pyramids
our sibling energies
turned to stone.

We dozed as acid rain
ate through bars
of triple prisons

where we waited
in separate caskets
for a prince on horseback

But now three feathers
tickle our crusted eyelashes
and we smile our lids apart

Our arms reach out
to endless squares
to triangular grasslands

Our voices sing out
through Mississippi bottoms
above New Mexico peaks

calling, "Fruitful, yes
we must be
fruitful again."

Three Eagles

Capes—no, wing spans,
three sister eagles
crystallized
mid-takeoff
arthritic talons
pointed toward
the lunar eye.

Outstretched feathers,
moonlight's parallax
blow specter white
like Belgian lace
lifted by breeze
past open windows.

Pointed beaks witch
clouds for rain, for
glimmer of blinking
dots, dashes, signs
of skywritten telegrams:
REAP SPARKS STOP
BREAK GLASS STOP
SOAR AGAIN STOP

Modern Maturity

Mine is the age
of invisibility:
graying hair
bulging veins
wrinkled skin
widow's hump.

Tradition says
adjust, stare
straight ahead,
you sack of bones.

I protest:
I will stamp my foot,
I will demand
the black pupil,
the blue, brown
or green iris
set in white
give me its due

For it is in
reaping eyes
I sow myself.

Crossings

Last fall at retreat
you showed me cross-stitch,
a pattern of rainbow and hearts
on a blue sweatshirt.

Later you thanked me
said I led you back
to needlework after months
away from lacing thread
through counted holes;
your pattern now,
a unicorn stitched
for Christmas gifts.

As you spoke your hands
and your mouth quivered,
eyes shrouded with tears.

On Monday I went to phone
you but I dreaded the knots,
friendship's ugly underside,
so I put it off, cross-stitched
rainbows and hearts instead.

You died that night.

[2]Wired Lovers

She:	He:
Beamed iris	Jaded queen
forehead grooving	whirling disc
word processing	daughter of the eye's
evaporator of evil	galvanic furnace
I flip into	mosaic
Vulcanic fire	means more
latent heat	pressure more
kinetic energy	vapors
I need you	co-processor
to interface	crunching bits
to harmonize	synchronizing signals
to multiply	shifting bytes
two programs	multiplexing
pulsating	E I E I/O

---

[2] Code: read horizontally (beamed iris jaded queen, forehead ...) or as two columns (beamed iris, forehead grooving ... ; and jaded queen, whirling disc ...).

Capitulation

A bumblebee invades
my honeybee hive.

My arms flail like stumps,
feet with fallen arches
stomp painfully,
my bald head nods,
my torso collapses
and I fall flat.

The bumblebee dives
at me, hates the ground,
so flies off to find
a higher place.

Agoraphobia

She peeks through blinds,
checks right, then left
around the front door.

Taking car keys
in one hand and the knob
in the other, she cracks
the door ajar and sighs.

Her chest rises and swells
as she pulls the door open
to see out farther
down the curving concrete.

She leans out, looks around
the door jamb and beyond
the outer facings, her head
swiveling, jerking side to side.

Eyes wide, she steps out over
the threshold and on down
the path, listening for sounds
not her own, shoes scraped,
shrubbery snapped, leaves
molested, rocks crushed.

Reaching her parked car,
she peers through windows,
checks floorboards front, back,
and seeing nothing unexpected,
unlocks the front door,

Enters the driver's seat,
shuts and locks the door,
fastens seat belts, inserts key,

starts the motor, and drives off.

On the roadway, wheels flap
as fear coils down for a wary nap.

Office Worker

You with drooped eye,
etched forehead,
handler of coffee
and office seething,
I hail you, brave worker.

You exude
pressured hours
of word processing
telephone answering
office regulating

Here children do not fit
spouses do not fit
and bosses neither
see the flame
nor lower the heat.

Yet joy distills in you
as a teapot whistles
until its essence,
lifted from fire,
reposes in its vessel.

Judith went back to Bethulia and lived on her estate. In her time she was famous throughout the whole country. She had many suitors; but she remained unmarried all her life after her husband Manasses died and was gathered to his fathers. Her fame continued to increase; and she lived on in her husband's house until she was a hundred and five years old. She gave her maid her liberty. She died in Bethulia and was buried in the same tomb as her husband Manasses, and Israel observed mourning for her for seven years. Before her death she divided her property among all those who were most closely related to her husband Manasses, and among her own nearest relations.

No one dared to threaten the Israelites again in Judith's lifetime, or for a long time after her death.

The Book of Judith 16: 21-25, NEB

Judith's Lament

Manasses, my love,
at night I feel you
carry me to sleep
with barley chaff
clinging to your skin

I see your tanned face
in the fields, the sun
boring through
your black curls
servants lifting you,
carrying you through ripe
grain, your once hot skin
cool to my touch,
eyes hooded,
breath still.

Your bones whiten
on the plains between
Dothan and Belamon

Other men pursue me
but I will never marry;
I fast and pray in
my shelter by the wall

One day I'll join you
chaste and pure
in His holy kingdom
Manasses, my love.

Prayer

Source of power
who breathes tones
through pipes of earth

Connector of the universe
who plugs our prongs
into the ancient currents

Ruler of destiny
who boots the flow
of sap in the maple tree

Spirit of fire
who lights the flash
that sparks ideas

Savior of souls
who leads the plunge
from darkness to light

Look on us now
and have mercy on us,
for we misuse your gifts.

Grant us forgiveness,
and keep us attuned
to your will, dear Lord.

Judith Rader Snyder

ABOUT THE AUTHOR

Judith Rader Snyder grew up on a farm in southern Indiana, the daughter of Owen and Kathleen Rader. She has a B.S. degree in music and English from Indiana State University. After marriage to Joseph Snyder, she moved to Houston, Texas, where she taught music in the public schools and raised two daughters, Marian and Gwen. An M.S. degree in literature earned at the University of Houston Clear Lake led her to teach English at San Jacinto Junior College. At the present time, she is a lay pastor candidate for the Presbyterian Church (U.S.A.). She is a published writer who writes poetry, short stories, and plays. Her favorite activities are worship, singing, reading, and family gatherings, where she enjoys the company of her eight grandchildren.

Printed in the United States
5090